He Says I Am . . .

30-DAY IDENTITY JOURNAL FOR YOUNG WOMEN OF FAITH

This Journal Belongs to:

_____

<u>Reference</u>

Holy Bible: Amplified Version. (1965). Zondervan House Publishing

WWW.FACEBOOK.COM/ATTHETABLECOMMUNICATION

ISBN:978-1-7354056-0-5

For More information, to order bulk copies, or event bookings, Please contact:
At The Table Communication, LLC.
atthetablecommnication@gmail.com

PRINTED IN U.S.A.

He Says I Am . . .

31-DAY IDENTITY JOURNAL FOR YOUNG WOMEN OF FAITH

Beloved of God,

One of the most foundational life questions that we all seek an answer to is "Who am I?" At some point in our lives, there is an awareness of a longing for understanding and insight into who we are at a deep, intimate level. Some may ask after an experience of loss in life, major transition, or after a defeat or failure. Others ask the question internally because they are keenly self-aware and desire to know more about themselves. No matter how it comes to you, the fact is that you have set out on a journey to discover more about yourself.

There is a beautiful message that I want to share with you. God has not hidden anything from you, that concerns you. Nothing. He has left His Word and clues in your spirit that answer what you seek.

This journal is designed to take you on a short, but enlightening look inside the mind and heart of God, concerning you. You see, God is a creator. The very first thing that He did in Genesis 1:1 was create. He created what He had envisioned in His mind before creation. Ephesians 1:4 declares that he created us in Himself before the foundation of the world. Everything that God created began with a thought. He made everything from within Himself, including you. He decided, upon His own counsel and that of Christ and Holy Spirit, that He would create mankind (us) in His image. Say what? Yes!

In Genesis 1:26, He decided to create humankind to be an image, or visual representation of, Himself. You see, Adam knew that His identity was in God. He walked in it every day. When sin entered the earth, Adam forfeited His identity and purpose over to the enemy. Christ came to restore us back to our original selves and purpose, in the image of God. Your creator knows EVERYTHING about you. You represent Him and cannot be separated from Him.

For some, this will be an introduction, while for others it will be a reminder that we are who He says we are.

- Rachelle L. Lawson

P.S. Download your FREE daily audio notes at bit.ly/Hesaysiam

Day One

I am intentionally made by the All Knowing God.

Psalm 139:14-15 Amplified

14*I will give thanks and praise to You, for I am fearfully and wonderfully made; Wonderful are Your works, And my soul knows it very well.*

15*My frame was not hidden from You, When I was being formed in secret, And intricately and skillfully formed [as if embroidered with many colors] in the depths of the earth.*

Read the entire 139 chapter of Psalm for more insight.

Write your own prayer in reference to how He knows you.

_____

_____

_____

_____

_____

_____

_____

_____

_____

_____

_____

_____

_____

_____

Day Two

I am loved, chosen, justified, sanctified, predestined and glorified by God.

Romans 8:29-30 Amplified

29 For those whom He foreknew [and loved and chose beforehand], He also predestined to be conformed to the image of His Son [and ultimately share in His complete sanctification] so that He would be the firstborn [the most beloved and honored] among many believers.

30 And those whom He predestined, He also called; and those whom He called, He also justified [declared free of the guilt of sin]; and those whom He justified, He also glorified [raising them to a heavenly dignity].

Date_____

Is there anything else in God's creation more treasured as you?

_____
_____
_____
_____
_____
_____
_____
_____
_____
_____
_____
_____
_____
_____
_____
_____

Day Three

I am created and designed by God.

Jeremiah 1:5 Amplified

5"*Before I formed you in the womb I knew you [and approved of you as My chosen instrument], And before you were born I consecrated you [to Myself as My own]; I have appointed you as a prophet to the nations.*"

How does this understanding
impact you and your life?

_____

_____

_____

_____

_____

_____

_____

_____

_____

_____

_____

_____

_____

_____

Day Four

I am planted and watered in God's Kingdom for service with Him.

Corinthians 3:9 Amplified

8 He who plants and he who waters are one [in importance and esteem, working toward the same purpose]; but each will receive his own reward according to his own labor.

9 For we are God's fellow workers [His servants working together]; you are God's cultivated field [His garden, His vineyard], God's building.

Teamwork makes the dream work.
How do you work with God?

_____

_____

_____

_____

_____

_____

_____

_____

_____

_____

_____

_____

_____

_____

Day Five

I am the light of the world.

Matthew 5:14 Amplified

14 *"You are the light of [Christ to] the world. A city set on a hill cannot be hidden;*

Just as Christ is the light, you are the light also. The world is desperate for your light to illuminate the hope of the Gospel.

Shine bright! The world cannot see clearly without you!

How do you shine your bright
light in your circle of influence?

_____

_____

_____

_____

_____

_____

_____

_____

_____

_____

_____

_____

_____

_____

_____

_____

Day Six

I am blessed with ALL spiritual blessings.

Ephesians 1:3 Amplified

³ Blessed and worthy of praise be the God and Father of our Lord Jesus Christ, who has blessed us with every spiritual blessing in the heavenly realms in Christ,

Date_____

*In what areas of your life do you
see the manifestation of blessings?*

_____
_____
_____
_____
_____
_____
_____
_____
_____
_____
_____
_____
_____
_____
_____
_____

Day Seven

I am divinely blessed.

Psalm 103:2 Amplified

*2 Bless and affectionately praise the Lord, O my soul,
And do not forget any of His benefits;
3 Who forgives all your sins,
Who heals all your diseases;
4 Who redeems your life from the pit,
Who crowns you [lavishly] with lovingkindness and
tender mercy;
5 Who satisfies your years with good things,
So that your youth is renewed like the [soaring] eagle.*

Date_____

In sad, difficult, or overwhelming
times, how can this support you?

_____
_____
_____
_____
_____
_____
_____
_____
_____
_____
_____
_____
_____
_____
_____

Day Eight

I am saved by grace through faith.

Ephesians 2:8 Amplified

8*For it is by grace [God's remarkable compassion and favor drawing you to Christ] that you have been saved [actually delivered from judgment and given eternal life] through faith. And this [salvation] is not of yourselves [not through your own effort], but it is the [undeserved, gracious] gift of God;*

Date_____

In what specific areas of your life have you been saved? Be specific.

_____

_____

_____

_____

_____

_____

_____

_____

_____

_____

_____

_____

_____

_____

_____

_____

_____

Day Nine

I am anointed.

I John 2:20 Amplified

20 But you have an anointing from the Holy One [you have been set apart, specially gifted and prepared by the Holy Spirit], and all of you know [the truth because He teaches us, illuminates our minds, and guards us from error].

Date_____

The anointing teaches us all truth. What truths have you learned?

_____

_____

_____

_____

_____

_____

_____

_____

_____

_____

_____

_____

_____

_____

Day Ten

I am delivered from darkness.

Colossians 1:13 Amplified

13 *For He has rescued us and has drawn us to Himself from the dominion of darkness, and has transferred us to the kingdom of His beloved Son,*

You are no longer a slave to darkness, but free! Rejoice!

_____

_____

_____

_____

_____

_____

_____

_____

_____

_____

_____

_____

_____

_____

Day Eleven

I am fruitful and prosperous.

Psalm 1:3 Amplified

₃ *And he will be like a tree firmly planted [and fed] by streams of water, Which yields its fruit in its season; Its leaf does not wither; And in whatever he does, he prospers [and comes to maturity].*

Date_____

What things in your life depend
on your fruit & prosperity?

_____
_____
_____
_____
_____
_____
_____
_____
_____
_____
_____
_____
_____
_____
_____

Day Twelve

I am rich and abundantly blessed.

II Corinthians 8:9 Amplified

[9] For you are recognizing [more clearly] the grace of our Lord Jesus Christ [His astonishing kindness, His generosity, His gracious favor], that though He was rich, yet for your sake He became poor, so that by His poverty you might become rich (abundantly blessed).

Date_____

Identify at least one area of your life that is richly blessed.

_____

_____

_____

_____

_____

_____

_____

_____

_____

_____

_____

_____

_____

_____

_____

_____

Day Thirteen

I am a living stone in God's house.

I Peter 2:5 Amplified

[5] *You [believers], like living stones, are being built up into a spiritual house for a holy and dedicated priesthood, to offer spiritual sacrifices [that are] acceptable and pleasing to God through Jesus Christ.*

God chose you to be a part of His house. A perfectly imperfect stone.

_____

_____

_____

_____

_____

_____

_____

_____

_____

_____

_____

_____

_____

Day Fourteen

I am prosperous in all ways.

III John 1:2 Amplified

2 Beloved, I pray that in every way you may succeed and prosper and be in good health [physically], just as [I know] your soul prospers [spiritually].

Reading God's word prospers our soul. All other prosperity follows.

_____

_____

_____

_____

_____

_____

_____

_____

_____

_____

_____

_____

_____

_____

_____

Day Fifteen

I am chosen by God.

I Peter 2:9 Amplified

⁹But you are a chosen people, a royal priesthood, a holy nation, God's special possession, that you may declare the praises of him who called you out of darkness into his wonderful light.

Date_____

How can your behavior mirror that
of God's special, royal people?

_____
_____
_____
_____
_____
_____
_____
_____
_____
_____
_____
_____
_____
_____
_____
_____

Day Sixteen

I am a new creation.

II Corinthians 5:17

17 Therefore if anyone is in Christ [that is, grafted in, joined to Him by faith in Him as Savior], he is a new creature [reborn and renewed by the Holy Spirit]; the old things [the previous moral and spiritual condition] have passed away. Behold, new things have come [because spiritual awakening brings a new life].

What new truth about your identity will move you forward?

_____

_____

_____

_____

_____

_____

_____

_____

_____

_____

_____

_____

_____

_____

Day Seventeen

I am a child of the living God.

Romans 1:16 Amplified

16 The Spirit Himself testifies and confirms together with our spirit [assuring us] that we [believers] are children of God.

Our Father God is not necessarily like our natural father. How so?

_____

_____

_____

_____

_____

_____

_____

_____

_____

_____

_____

_____

_____

_____

_____

Day Eighteen

I am led by the Spirit of God.

Romans 8:14 Amplified

[14] For all who are allowing themselves to be led by the Spirit of God are sons of God.

How do you measure up in the
leading a life of obedience?

_____

_____

_____

_____

_____

_____

_____

_____

_____

_____

_____

_____

_____

_____

_____

_____

Day Nineteen

I am an overcomer.

Revelation 12:11 Amplified

[11] *And they overcame and conquered him because of the blood of the Lamb and because of the word of their testimony, for they did not love their life and renounce their faith even when faced with death.*

Life can get tough and adulting overrated, you can overcome.

_____
_____
_____
_____
_____
_____
_____
_____
_____
_____
_____
_____
_____
_____
_____

Day Twenty

I am the authority over the enemy.

Luke 10:19 Amplified

[19] *Listen carefully: I have given you authority [that you now possess] to tread on serpents and scorpions, and [the ability to exercise authority] over all the power of the enemy (Satan); and nothing will [in any way] harm you.*

In what areas of life do you find your biggest fight? Take it back!

_____

_____

_____

_____

_____

_____

_____

_____

_____

_____

_____

_____

_____

_____

_____

_____

Day Twenty-One

I am flourishing in my life.

Psalm 92:12-13 Amplified

12 The righteous will flourish like the date palm [long-lived, upright and useful]; They will grow like a cedar in Lebanon [majestic and stable].

13 Planted in the house of the Lord, They will flourish in the courts of our God.

Envision yourself living your most
ideal life. Describe it.

_____

_____

_____

_____

_____

_____

_____

_____

_____

_____

_____

_____

_____

_____

_____

_____

Day Twenty-Two

I am lacking nothing.

II Peter 1:3 Amplified

3 For His divine power has bestowed on us [absolutely] everything necessary for [a dynamic spiritual] life and godliness through true and personal knowledge of Him who called us by His own glory and excellence.

God is committed to you, His representative. Your needs are met.

_____

_____

_____

_____

_____

_____

_____

_____

_____

_____

_____

_____

_____

_____

Day Twenty-Three

I am Holy.

I Peter 1:14-16 Amplified

14 *[Live] as obedient children [of God]; do not be conformed to the evil desires which governed you in your ignorance [before you knew the requirements and transforming power of the good news regarding salvation].*
15 *But like the Holy One who called you, be holy yourselves in all your conduct [be set apart from the world by your godly character and moral courage];*
16 *because it is written, "You shall be holy (set apart), for I am holy."*

Recognize that you carry holiness and divinity within you. Be holy.

_____

_____

_____

_____

_____

_____

_____

_____

_____

_____

_____

_____

_____

_____

Day Twenty-Four

I am wise.

James 1:5 Amplified

[5] *If any of you lacks wisdom [to guide him through a decision or circumstance], he is to ask of [our benevolent] God, who gives to everyone generously and without rebuke or blame, and it will be given to him.*

Do you trust your inner voice? Be sensitive to the wisdom inside you.

_____

_____

_____

_____

_____

_____

_____

_____

_____

_____

_____

_____

_____

_____

_____

_____

Day Twenty-Five

I am able to fulfill my assignment with Christ.

Philippians 4:13 Amplified

[13] I can do all things [which He has called me to do] through Him who strengthens and empowers me [to fulfill His purpose—I am self-sufficient in Christ's sufficiency; I am ready for anything and equal to anything through Him who infuses me with inner strength and confident peace.]

God empowers us to do all He assigns us, with Him. Use Him.

_____

_____

_____

_____

_____

_____

_____

_____

_____

_____

_____

_____

_____

_____

Day Twenty-Six

I am a making disciples of Christ.

Matthew 28:19 Amplified

¹⁹ Go therefore and make disciples of all the
nations [help the people to learn of Me, believe in Me,
and obey My words], baptizing them in the name of
the Father and of the Son and of the Holy Spirit,

Be bold in sharing Christ. Their lives and eternity depends on it.

Day Twenty-Seven

I am an heir of God and Christ.

Romans 8:17 Amplified

17 And if [we are His] children, [then we are His] heirs also: heirs of God and fellow heirs with Christ [sharing His spiritual blessing and inheritance], if indeed we share in His suffering so that we may also share in His glory.

Date_____

How do you feel knowing that you have a wealthy inheritance?

_____
_____
_____
_____
_____
_____
_____
_____
_____
_____
_____
_____
_____
_____
_____

Day Twenty-Eight

I am an heir of the blessing of Abraham.

Galatians 3:13-14 Amplified

[13] *Christ purchased our freedom and redeemed us from the curse of the Law and its condemnation by becoming a curse for us—for it is written, "Cursed is everyone who hangs [crucified] on a tree (cross)"—* [14] *in order that in Christ Jesus the blessing of Abraham might also come to the Gentiles, so that we would all receive [the realization of] the promise of the [Holy] Spirit through faith.*

How would you describe God's love in your current season?

_____

_____

_____

_____

_____

_____

_____

_____

_____

_____

_____

_____

_____

_____

_____

Day Twenty-Nine

I am healed.

I Peter 2:2 Amplified

*24 He personally carried our sins in His body on
the cross [willingly offering Himself on it, as on an
altar of sacrifice], so that we might die to sin
[becoming immune from the penalty and power of sin]
and live for righteousness; for by His wounds you [who
believe] have been healed.*

Healing is not only physical. It is emotional, mental, or financial.

_____

_____

_____

_____

_____

_____

_____

_____

_____

_____

_____

_____

_____

_____

Day Thirty

I am walking by faith daily.

II Corinthians 5:7 Amplified

17 *for we walk by faith, not by sight [living our lives in a manner consistent with our confident belief in God's promises]*

Identify ways in which you can please God by walking in faith.

_____
_____
_____
_____
_____
_____
_____
_____
_____
_____
_____
_____
_____
_____
_____
_____
_____
_____

Reflections

ABOUT THE CREATOR

Rachelle Lawson is a two-time Phi Theta Kappa Teaching Excellence Award- Winning educator, motivational teacher, speaker, and clarity and relationship coach for young women. She is the Founder and Principal of At The Table Communication, LLC, whose mission is to support the preservation of families through education, leadership, and personal development of young women ages 18-30. Her superpowers are her God-given grace toward relationships, unique storytelling ability and her person-centered approach to life and leadership. In 2019, Rachelle released her first book entitled <u>Girl, Get Yo' Life! A Young Woman's Guide to Life and Relationships that Win.</u> She was motivated to write this book as a response to a cultural need. In addition, she has also develeped an online course and coaching program to support young women on the path to self discovery, purpose and healthy relationships. Rachelle is a native of Ohio where she resides with her family.

Let's Connect!

o Visit my social media
www.facebook.com/atthetablecommun
cation
@girl_getyolife on **Instagram**
Rachelle Lawson on **LinkedIn**

o Download , listen, and share my FREE
podcast: *Rachelle's Corner* on Spotify,
Apple Podcasts, Google Podcasts,
PocketCasts and Anchor

o Join my FREE Facebook group at
www.facebook.com/groups/empoweredt
othrivelife/

o Get on path by joining my online course:
www.thrivinglife.today/offer

o Book Me for speaking or workshop facilitation
by contacting:
atthetablecommunication@gmail.com

Other Books by Rachelle

*Girl, Get Yo' Life! A Young Woman's Guide to Life and Relationships that
Win*

*Girl, Get Yo' Life! A Young Woman's Guide to Life and Relationships that
Win Workbook*

CPSIA information can be obtained
at www.ICGtesting.com
Printed in the USA
LVHW050109231220
674889LV00015B/1433